D1329060

Love

A BOOK OF QUOTATIONS

Love

A BOOK OF QUOTATIONS

Edited by Ann Braybrooks

DOVER PUBLICATIONS, INC.
Mineola, New York

Copyright
Copyright © 2012 by Dover Publications, Inc.
All rights reserved.

Bibliographical Note
Love: A Book of Quotations is a new work, first published by Dover Publications, Inc.,
in 2012.

Library of Congress Cataloging-in-Publication Data
Love : a book of quotations / [edited by] Ann Braybrooks.
    p. cm.
 Summary: "'A heart set on love will do no wrong,' declared Confucius. This
compact gift book features an international assortment of romantic ruminations
from ancient and modern philosophers, playwrights, poets, novelists, commentators,
critics, and actors. Wise, worldly, sentimental, and cynical, the quotes will touch
hearts all year long"— Provided by publisher.
   ISBN-13: 978-0-486-48131-9 (pbk.)
   ISBN-10: 0-486-48131-X
      1. Love—Quotations, maxims, etc. I. Braybrooks, Ann.
 PN6084.L6L58325 2012
 302.3—dc22

                                                                    2011019593

Book Design by Paula Goldstein, Blue Bungalow Design

Manufactured in the United States by Courier Corporation
48131X01
www.doverpublications.com

Introduction

Love: A Book of Quotations is a tender treasury of thoughts and feelings about romantic love, as observed and experienced over the centuries by men and women who cared to express themselves on a subject that delighted, inspired, perplexed, depressed, or infuriated them.

The selections included here, by authors ranging from an anonymous ancient Egyptian to a twentieth-century Irish Nobel Prize winner, reveal a range of temperaments and attitudes. While many quotations focus on the more interesting, joyful, and hopeful aspects of love, unrequited love and lost love are not ignored. Among the empirical analyses, heartfelt hymns, and sentimental valentines are also pleas, complaints, and laments.

While most authors agree that love is powerful, and that almost nothing can contain or conceal it, they disagree on other matters. Is it possible to love at first sight? Does absence contribute to love's renewal or its destruction? Is love blind? Is the soul most important to love, or the body? Both?

Some call love a religion. Yet to more than one observer, love is far from heavenly and can cause "an age of pain," according to George Granville (1666–1734/5). Authors such as Marie de France, Barnabe Googe, and Thomas Hardy weigh in on love's grief and cruelty.

Thankfully, declarations of wonder, ecstasy, tenderness, and gratitude appear in the words of John Donne, Anne Bradstreet, Anne Finch, D. H. Lawrence, and others. The fragments and passages in this book provide just a glimmer of their sublimity. There is much to enjoy.

* * *

This collection is arranged alphabetically by author, and most quotations are taken from books and poems. Of the 375 quotations here, a number of them contain dashes and exclamation marks. The exclamation mark was introduced into printing in the fifteenth century; and for centuries, authors and editors embraced it. Recently, the use of an exclamation mark to indicate astonishment or admiration has been ridiculed, and it appears more commonly in personal correspondence and on the Internet than in traditionally published material. Readers can decide for themselves if they like the extra flourish.

Eliza Acton

I love thee, as the glad bird loves
  The freedom of its wing,
On which delightedly it moves
  In wildest wandering.

Joseph Addison

Love is not to be reasoned down, or lost
In high ambition, or a thirst of greatness:
'Tis second life; it grows into the soul,
Warms every vein, and beats in every pulse.

. . . thy words shoot through my heart,
Melt my resolves, and turn me all to love.

Louisa May Alcott

Love is a great beautifier.

The best of us have a spice of perversity in us,
especially when we are young and in love.

Sherwood Anderson

There's a kind of girl you see just once in your
life, and if you don't get busy and make hay, then
you're gone for good and all and might as well go
jump off a bridge.

Anonymous (Egyptian)

O, hurry to look at your love!
    Be like horses charging in battle,
Like a gardener up with the sun
    burning to watch his prize bud open.

Anonymous (English)

He that hath love in his breast hath spurs at his heels.

Anonymous (Greek)

I will make you an altar upon a high peak in a far seen place, and will sacrifice rich offerings to you at all seasons.

Edwin Arnold

One can be a soldier without dying,
And lover without sighing.

Somewhere there waiteth in this world
   of ours
For one lone soul another lonely soul,
Each chasing each through all the weary hours
And meeting strangely at one sudden goal.

Margot Asquith

In spite of what you say, some man might fall in
love with me, you know!

Jane Austen

All the privilege I claim for my own sex (it is not a very enviable one: you need not covet it), is that of loving longest, when existence or when hope is gone!

I cannot fix on the hour, or the spot, or the look, of the words, which laid the foundation. It is too long ago. I was in the middle before I knew that I *had* begun.

I wonder who first discovered the efficacy of poetry in driving away love!

Jane Austen

It is always incomprehensible to a man that a woman should ever refuse an offer of marriage.

It is not time or opportunity that is to determine intimacy;—it is disposition alone. Seven years would be insufficient to make some people acquainted with each other, and seven days are more than enough for others.

Such a change in a man of so much pride excited not only astonishment but gratitude—for to love, ardent love, it must be attributed; and, as such, its impression on her was of a sort to be encouraged, as by no means unpleasing, though it could not be exactly defined.

To be sure you know no actual good of me—but nobody thinks of *that* when they fall in love.

Alfred Austin

They do not love who give the body and keep
The heart ungiven; nor they who yield the soul,
And guard the body. Love doth give the whole;
Its range being high as heaven, as ocean deep,
Wide as the realms of air or planet's curving
    sweep.

Honoré de Balzac

Love is the poetry of the senses. It has the destiny of all that which is great in man and of all that which proceeds from his thought. Either it is sublime, or it is not.

There are few things inexhaustible in a lover: goodness, gracefulness and delicacy.

Talent in love, as in every other art, consists in the power of forming a conception combined with the power of carrying it out.

When women love, they forgive everything, even our crimes; when they do not love, they cannot forgive anything—not even our virtues.

J. M. Barrie

Love, it is said, is blind, but love is not blind. It is an extra eye, which shows us what is most worthy of regard. To see the best is to see most clearly, and it is the lover's privilege.

Charles Baudelaire

There are women who inspire one with the desire to woo them and win them; but she makes one wish to die slowly beneath her steady gaze.

Samuel Alfred Beadle

And when she turns her dimpled cheek
    Toward me for a kiss,
I lose expression—cannot speak—
    And take all there is of bliss.

Henry Ward Beecher

Young love is a flame; very pretty, often very hot and fierce, but still only light and flickering. The love of the older and disciplined heart is as coals, deep-burning, unquenchable.

Aphra Behn

Come, my eternal pleasure—Each moment of the happy lover's hour, is worth an age of dull and common life.

Oh what a dear ravishing thing is the beginning of an Amour!

Frances Boothby

You powerful Gods! If I must be
An injured offering to Love's deity,
Grant my revenge, this plague on men,
That woman may ne'er love again.

James Boswell

A gentleman who had been very unhappy in
marriage married immediately after his wife died;
Johnson said it was the triumph of hope over
experience.

Caroline Bowles

It is not love that steals the heart from love;
'Tis the hard world, and its perplexing cares;
Its petrifying selfishness, its pride,
Its low ambition, and its paltry aims.

Caroline Bowles

> Never tell me of loving by measure and weight,
>   As one's merits may lack or abound;
> As if love could be carried to market like skate
>   And cheapened for so much a-pound.

Anne Bradstreet

> If ever two were one, then surely we.
> If ever man were loved by wife, then thee;
> If ever wife was happy in a man,
> Compare with me, ye women, if you can.

Charlotte Brontë

> I don't call you handsome, sir, though I love you
> most dearly—far too dearly to flatter you.
> Don't flatter me.

Elizabeth Barrett Browning

And what I *feel*, across the inferior features
Of what I *am*, doth flash itself, and show
How that great work of Love enhances Nature's.

. . . But I look on thee—on thee—
Beholding, besides love, the end of love,
Hearing oblivion beyond memory;
As one who sits and gazes from above,
Over the rivers to the bitter sea.

I love thee freely, as men strive for right
I love thee purely, as they turn from praise
I love thee with the passion put to use
In my old griefs, and my childhood's faith.

Robert Browning

I hopeless, I the loveless, hope and love.
Wiser and better, know me now, not when
You loved me as I was.

Edward George Bulwer-Lytton

It seems to me that the coming of love is like the coming of spring—the date is not to be reckoned by the calendar.

Love sacrifices all things
To bless the thing it loves!

Of all the agonies of life, that which is most poignant and harrowing—that which for the time annihilates reason, and leaves our whole organization one lacerated, mangled heart—is the conviction that we have been deceived where we placed all the trust of love.

Robert Burns

For my own part, I never had the least thought, or inclination of turning poet, 'till I got once heartily in love; and then rhyme and song were, in a manner, the spontaneous language of my heart.

To see her is to love her,
    And love but her forever;
For nature made her what she is,
    And ne'er made sic anither!

We may be poor—Robie and I,
    Light is the burden luve lays on;
Content and luve brings peace and joy,
    What mair hae queens upon a throne?

Robert Burton

Shall I say, most part of a lover's life is full of agony, anxiety, fear and grief, complaints, sighs, suspicions, and cares (heigh-ho my heart is woe), full of silence and irksome solitariness?

Love is a delectation of the heart, occasioned by some apparently good, amiable, and fair object, the favor or possession of which the mind ardently wishes to win and seeks to enjoy.

No cord or cable can draw so forcibly, or bind so fast, as this charming passion can do with only a single thread; for when formed on just and rational principles, it possesses the virtues of the adamant, and leads to an inexhaustible source of increasing pleasure.

Robert Burton

The temporary absence of those whom we love and esteem casts a sorrowful gloom over the mind and gives a painful uneasiness to the heart.

Lord Byron (George Gordon)

Man's love is of man's life a thing apart;
'Tis woman's whole existence: man may range
The court, camp, church, the vessel, and the mart;
Sword, gown, gain, glory, offer in exchange
Pride, fame, ambition, to fill up his heart,
And few there are whom these cannot estrange.

Why did she love him? Curious fool—
Be still:
Is human love the growth of human
will?

James Branch Cabell

All we poets write a deal about love: but none of us may grasp the word's full meaning until he reflects that this is a passion mighty enough to induce a woman to put up with him.

Love's sowing is more agreeable than love's harvest.

Yet even now I love you more than I love books and indolence and flattery and the charitable wine which cheats me into a favorable opinion of myself. What more can an old poet say?

Luís Vaz de Camões

'Tis nothing to me, my Mother—
What love commands I'll do;
I'll go with my mariner, Mother,
And be a mariner, too.

Thomas Campion

If all would lead their lives in love like me,
Then bloody swords and armor should not
   be;
Nor drum nor trumpet peaceful sleeps should
   move
Unless alarm came from the camp of love . . .

Though love and all his pleasures are but
   toys,
They shorten tedious nights.

Thomas Carew

Either extreme, of love or hate,
Is sweeter than a calm estate.

No tears, Celia, now shall win
My resolved heart to return;
I have searched thy soul within
And find nought but pride and scorn.

Thomas Carlyle

Love is not altogether a delirium, yet it has many
points in common therewith.

Giacomo Casanova

She kissed me at every opportunity, called me her
darling boy, her joy, and as the present moment
is the only real thing in this life, I enjoyed her
love, I was pleased with her caresses, and put
away all ideas of the dreadful future, which has
only one certainty—death, *ultima linea rerum*.

Giacomo Casanova

I resolved never to abandon her, and I did so in all sincerity; was I not in love?

I would have nothing to do with that Platonic affection devoid of love, but I leave you go guess what my maxim would be.

To love and enjoy; to enjoy and love. Turn and turn about.

Your asking me so freely for what you want is a true proof of your love; where confidence dwells not there is no love.

We swore to be faithful forever, and our oaths were sincere, as ardent lovers' oaths always are. But they are nought unless they are sealed by destiny, and that no mortal mind may know.

Donna Castelloza

The world asserts, it ill becomes our sex to show their love, when it is ill received; but those who say this, know not what love is; those who can practice it, have never loved!

Compared to yours, all other love is a shadow.

Gaius Catullus

Let us live, my Lesbia, and love, and value at a penny all the talk of crabbed old men.

Miguel de Cervantes

"That's the nature of women," cried Don Quixote, "not to love when we love them, and to love when we love them not."

Nicolas de Chamfort

Love gives greater pleasure than marriage for the same reason that romances are more amusing than history.

Love resembles epidemic diseases: the more one fears them, the more liable is one to infection.

When women forget themselves it is never for love of an honest man but of a rascal.

Anton Chekhov

In the guidebooks it says that a love affair is an essential condition for a tour in Italy. Well, hang them all! I am ready for anything. If there must be a love affair, so be it.

My ideal is to be idle and to love a plump girl.

Anton Chekhov

> To marry is interesting only for love; to marry
> a girl simply because she is nice is like buying
> something one does not want at the bazaar solely
> because it is of good quality.

Samuel Taylor Coleridge

> Alas, they had been friends in youth;
> But whispering tongues can poison truth;
> And constancy lives in realms above;
> And life is thorny; and youth is vain;
> And to be wroth with one we love
> Doth work like madness in the brain.
>
> All thoughts, all passions, all delights,
> Whatever stirs this mortal frame,
> All are but ministers of Love,
> And feed his sacred flame.

Sir Arthur Conan Doyle

I did not know how easy it is to be noble
when some one else takes it for granted that
one will be so; or how wide and interesting
life becomes when viewed by four eyes
instead of two.

It was all love on my side, and all good
comradeship and friendship on hers. When
we parted she was a free woman, but I could
never again be a free man.

Confucius

A heart set on love will do no wrong.

Wisdom delights in water; love delights in hills. Wisdom is stirring; love is quiet. Wisdom enjoys life; love grows old.

Joseph Conrad

. . . woe to the man whose heart has not learned while young to hope, to love—and to put its trust in life!

Pierre Corneille

Love rules the earth, subjects the heavens; kings are at his feet; he controls the gods.

Abraham Cowley

. . . and if I were ever in love again (which is a
great passion, and therefore, I hope, I have done
with it), it would be, I think, with prettiness,
rather than with majestical beauty.

William Cowper

What is there in the vale of life
Half so delightful as a wife,
When friendship, love and peace combine
To stamp the marriage-bond divine?

Charles Dickens

Love, however, is very materially assisted by a
warm and active imagination, which has a long
memory, and will thrive, for a considerable time,
on very slight and sparing food.

Emily Dickinson

Futile the winds
To a heart in port,—
Done with the compass,
Done with the chart.

Heart, we will forget him!
You and I, tonight!
You may forget the warmth he gave,
I will forget the light.

It's all I have to bring to-day,
This, and my heart beside,
This, and my heart, and all the fields,
And all the meadows wide.

Emily Dickinson

So we must keep apart,
You there, I here,
With just the door ajar
That oceans are . . .

Benjamin Disraeli

The magic of first love is the ignorance that it
can ever end.

We are all born for love. It is the principle of
existence and its only end.

John Donne

And now good-morrow to our waking souls,
Which watch not one another out of fear;
For love all love of other sights controls
And makes one little room an everywhere.

John Donne

I am two fools, I know,
For loving, and for saying so
    In whining poetry.

Gems which you women use
Are like Atlanta's ball cast in men's views;
That, when a fool's eye lighteth on a gem,
His earthly soul might court that, not them.

William Douglas

Her voice is low and sweet;
And she's a' the world to me;
And for bonnie Annie Laurie
I'd lay me doune and die.

John Dryden

But of my heart I now a present make;
And give it to you, ere it be yours to take.
Accept it as when early fruit we send:
And let the rareness the small gift commend.

For, Heaven be thanked, we live in such an age,
When no man dies for love, but on the stage.

Kings fight for kingdoms, madmen for applause;
But love for love alone, that crowns the lover's
    cause.

Love never fails to master what he finds,
But works a different way in different minds;
The fool enlightens, and the wise he blinds.

Love reckons hours for months, and days for
    years;
And every little absence is an age.

Charles Pinot Duclos

I had read some few romances, and believed myself in love; the pleasure, the honor of being distinguished, nay caressed, by an amiable woman, added to the impression which jewels, dress, and perfumes naturally make on the mind of a young man, and, above all, a fine neck, (and madam Valcourt's was divinely beautiful) awakened every source of passion in me.

To blame a youth for being love-sick is like reproaching a man because he has bad health.

Alexandre Dumas

. . . love lends wings to our desires.

I was already in the condition of Moliere's lovers who always get as far as the door, but who never make up their minds to cross the threshold.

It cannot be wondered at that his mind, generally so courageous, but now disturbed by the two strongest passions, love and fear, was weakened even to the indulgence of superstitious thoughts.

Alexandre Dumas

> . . .The only definite incontestably real actual thing was that during the last quarter of an hour I had fallen in love.
>
> With whom?
>
> With no one as yet . . . But with Love.

Paul Laurence Dunbar

Because you love me I have much achieved,
Had you despised me then I must have failed,
But since I knew you trusted and believed,
I could not disappoint you and so prevailed.

Tell your love where the roses blow,
And the hearts of the lilies quiver,
Not in the city's gleam and glow,
But down by a half-sunned river.

They loved, and loving they lingered long,
For to love is sweet, so sweet.

T. S. Eliot

> And would it have been worth it, after all,
> After the cups, the marmalade, the tea,
> Among the porcelain, among some talk of you
>   and me,
> Would it have been worth while,
> To have bitten off the matter with a smile,
> To have squeezed the universe into a ball . . .

Ralph Waldo Emerson

> And what is specially true of love is, that it is a
> state of extreme impressionability; the lover has
> more senses and finer senses than others; his
> eye and ear are telegraphs; he reads omens on
> the flower, and cloud, and face, and form, and
> gesture, and he reads them aright.

Ralph Waldo Emerson

For it is a fire that, kindling its first embers in the narrow nook of a private bosom, caught from a wandering spark out of another private heart, glows and enlarges until it warms and beams upon multitudes of men and women, upon the universal heart of all, and so lights up the whole world and all nature with its generous flames.

Etienne

We always come back to our first loves.

Anne Finch

Love (if such a thing there be)
Is all despair, or ecstasy.

Anne Finch

Love, thou art best of human joys,
  Our chiefest happiness below;
All other pleasures are but toys,
Musick without thee is but noise,
  And beauty but an empty show.

This is to the crown and blessing of my life,
The much-loved husband of a happy wife;
To him, whose constant passion found the art
To win a stubborn and ungrateful heart,
And to the world, by tenderest proof discovers
They err, who say that husbands can't be lovers.

Bernard le Bovier de Fontenelle

I write to you, Madam, in a language which you know little of, as yet: But then to make you amends, I have chosen a subject to write upon which you will easily conceive. When I tell you that I think you the most amiable woman in the world, I believe you will have no need of an interpreter.

To be plain, I love you only because I know nobody at present that deserves so much to be beloved; and if ever I should find a person whose merit were greater than yours, you must no longer depend on my constancy.

Tenderness has also its value . . .

Or why do not a couple of lovers love both at once, and cease to love at the same time? I am so angry with Love that at this moment I wish he were exterminated out of this world.

Marie de France

But who may brag of patience when true love
Tortures without all cease?

Benjamin Franklin

Keep your eyes wide open before marriage; half
shut afterwards.

Love, cough, and a smoke can't well be hid.

Lovers, travelers, and poets will give money to be
heard.

Where there's marriage without love, there will
be love without marriage.

Robert Frost

Ah, when to the heart of man
    Was it ever less than a treason
To go with the drift of things,
    To yield with a grace to reason,
And bow and accept the end
    Of a love or a season?

And it seems like the time when after doubt
    Our love came back amain.
Oh, come forth into the storm and rout
    And be my love in the rain.

John Galsworthy

A marvelous speeder-up of Love is War.
What might have taken six months was thus
accomplished in three weeks.

John Galsworthy

Love is no hot-house flower, but a wild plant,
born of a wet night, born of an hour of sunshine;
sprung from wild seed, blown along the road by a
wild wind.

Johann Wolfgang von Goethe

A mere trifle is enough to amuse two lovers.

Frantic and passionate happiness, in which
we lose our own selves, will also darken the
reminiscence of those we love. But when you
are fully conscious and very tranquil, your mind
is open to a peculiar sympathy, and all dead
friendships and loves rise into life again.

In love all is risk.

Love and necessity are the best of masters.

Johann Wolfgang von Goethe

Love, charity, and science can alone make us happy and tranquil in this world of ours.

That is the true season of love, when we believe that we alone can love, that no one could ever have loved so before us and that no one will love in the same way after us.

We lose the best part of life if we are cut off from communication and sympathy. Sympathy is most needed when it is scarcely ever to be had—namely, in affairs of the heart.

Emma Goldman

If love does not know how to give and take without restriction, it is not love, but a transaction that never fails to lay stress on a plus and a minus.

Oliver Goldsmith

Love, when founded in the heart, will show itself
in a thousand unpremeditated sallies of fondness;
but every cool deliberate exhibition of the
passion only argues little understanding or great
insincerity.

Barnabe Googe

Two lines shall tell the grief that I by love sustain:
I burn, I flame, I faint, I freeze, of hell I feel the
pain.

George Granville

Here end my chains, and thralldom cease,
If not in joy, I'll live at least in peace:
Since for the pleasures of an hour,
We must endure an age of pain,
I'll be this abject thing no more.
Love, give me back my heart again.

George Granville

> . . . in vain from Fate we fly,
> For first, or last, as all must die;
> So 'tis as much decreed above,
> That first, or last, we all must love.

Hafez

In the book of the most skilful physician is to be found no chapter on love: O my heart, accustom thyself to suffering, and inquire not about the remedy.

In the game of love, there is need of patience.

Sweet are the garden, the rose, and the wine, but they would not be sweet without the company of my darling.

What necessity for a sword to slay the lover, when a glance can deprive him of half his life?

Hafez

Whither shall I go?—what shall I do?—to whom tell the condition of my heart? Who will do me justice?—who will repay me what I deserve for the pain of separation?

Thomas Hardy

For of all the miseries attaching to miserable love, the worst is the misery of thinking that the passion which is the cause of them all may cease.

How silly I was in my happiness when I thought I could trust you to always love me! I ought to have known that such as that was not for poor me. But I am sick at heart, not only for old times, but for the present. Think—think how it do hurt my heart not to see you ever—ever! Ah, if I could only make your dear heart ache one little minute of each day as mine does every day and all day long, it might lead you to show pity to your poor lonely one.

Thomas Hardy

> Love is long-suffering, brave,
> Sweet, prompt, precious as a jewel;
> But O, too, Love is cruel,
> Cruel as the grave.

Heinrich Heine

> I had a dream long since of Love's wild glow—
> Locks, mignonette and myrtle—all it teaches
> Of sweet, red kisses and of bitter speeches;
> Sad airs of sadder songs—long, long ago!

Robert Herrick

> Love is a circle that doth restless move
> In the same sweet eternity of love.
>
> Love's of itself too sweet; the best of all
> Is when love's honey has a dash of gall.

Robert Herrick

Thou art my life, my love, my heart,
    The very eyes of me:
And hast command of every part
    To live and die for thee.

You say to me-wards your affection's strong;
Pray love me little, so you love me long.

Hesiod

Do not let a flaunting woman coax and cozen
and deceive you: she is after your barn.

James Hogg

O, love, love, love!
    Love is like a dizziness,
It winna let a poor body
    Gang about his biziness!

Josiah Gilbert Holland

A woman in love is a very poor judge of character.

The heart is wiser than the intellect,
And works with swifter hands and surer feet
Toward wise conclusions.

Arsène Houssaye

When we cannot love the original, we love the likeness.

Victor Hugo

If you are stone, be loadstone; it you are plant, be sensitive; it you are man, be love.

Love is powerful enough to charge all nature with its messages.

Victor Hugo

Love partakes of the soul itself. It is of the same nature. Like it, it is a divine spark; like it, it is incorruptible, indivisible, imperishable.

The heart becomes heroic through passion.

Washington Irving

I profess not to know how women's hearts are wooed and won. To me they have always been matters of riddle and admiration.

Samuel Johnson

Lovers all but love disdain.

Those that have loved longest love best.

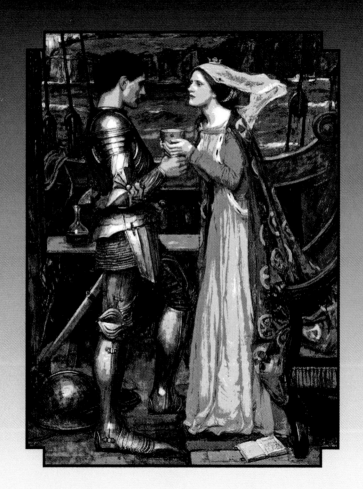

Ben Jonson

Drink to me only with thine eyes,
And I will pledge with mine;
Or leave a kiss within the cup,
And I'll not look for wine.

Give me a look, give me a face,
That makes simplicity a grace;
Robes loosely flowing, hair as free:
Such sweet neglect more taketh me
Than all the adulteries of art;
They strike mine eyes, but not my heart.

Joseph Joubert

He who cannot see the beautiful side is a bad painter, a bad friend, a bad lover; he cannot lift his mind and his heart so high as goodness.

Kalidasa

Ah! a lover's feelings betray themselves by his gestures.

John Keats

I almost wish we were butterflies and lived but three summer days—three such days with you I could fill with more delight than fifty common years could ever contain.

I wish you could invent some means to make me at all happy without you. Every hour I am more and more concentrated in you; everything else tastes like chaff in the mouth.

John Keats

Love is my religion.—I could die for that. I could die for you. My Creed is Love and you are its only tenet.

Ono no Komachi

A thing which fades
With no outward sign—
Is the flower
Of the heart of man
In this world!

Jean de La Bruyère

As long as love lasts, it feeds on itself, and sometimes by those very means which seem rather likely to extinguish it, such as caprice, severity, absence, jealousy.

Jean de La Bruyère

> If I were to admit that in the ebullitions of a violent passion one may love another person better than oneself, whom should I please most—those who love or those who are beloved?

> Sudden love takes the longest time to cured.

> We never love with all our heart and all our soul but once, and that is the first time we love. Subsequent inclinations are less instinctive.

Alphonse de Lamartine

> I did not know how I loved her,—whether it was pure companionship, friendship, love, habit, or all of these sentiments combined, that made up my affection for her.

Alphonse de Lamartine

I was at that ungrateful age when the spirit of levity and fashion makes a young man ashamed of the best sentiments of his soul, a cruel age when the grandest gifts of God—pure love, innocent affections—fall in the dust and are carried away in their bloom by the wind of the world.

To love for the sake of being loved is human, but to love for the sake of loving is angelic.

Letitia Elizabeth Landon

They parted as all lovers part;—
She with her wrong'd and breaking heart;
But he, rejoicing he is free,
    Bounds like a captive from his chain,
And willfully believing she
    Hath found her liberty again;
Or if dark thoughts will cross his mind,
They are but clouds before the wind.

Letitia Elizabeth Landon

Love is the least calculating of all dreamers.

Shame is the worst pang of unrequited affection.

By-the-by, what an ugly phrase—"making love" is—as if love were a dress or a pudding.

Idleness and vanity cause, in nine cases out of ten, that state of excitement which is called being in love.

Walter Savage Landor

Is it not in philosophy as in love? The more we have of it, and the less we talk about it, the better.

There are secrets which not even love should try to penetrate.

Francois, Duc de La Rochefoucauld

All the passions make us commit faults, but in love we are guilty of the most ridiculous ones.

In love, we often doubt of what we most believe.

It is impossible to love a second time those whom we have really ceased to love.

Love is one and the same in the original; but there are a thousand different copies of it.

No disguise can long conceal love where it is, nor feign where it is not.

The pleasure of loving is to love; we are much happier in the passion we feel than in that we excite.

There are many cures for love; not one of them infallible.

D. H. Lawrence

And at last I know my love for you is here,
I can see it all, it is whole like the twilight,
It is large, so large, I could not see it before
Because of the little lights and flickers and
    interruptions,
Troubles, anxieties and pains.

I learned it all from my Eve
    This warm, dumb wisdom.
She's a finer instructress than years;
She has taught my heart-strings to weave
Through the web of all laughter and tears.

D. H. Lawrence

I should like to drop
On the hay, with my head on her knee
And lie stone still, while she
Breathed quiet above me—we could stop
Till the stars came out to see.

Ninon de l'Enclos

I am frank, and I am quite sure if women would
be honest, they would soon confess that they
are not a bit more refined than men. Indeed, if
they saw in love only the pleasures of the soul,
if they hoped to please only by their mental
accomplishments and good character, honestly,
now, would they apply themselves with such
particular care to please by the charms of their
person?

Ninon de l'Enclos

I have always contended that love never dies
from desire but often from indigestion.

Love is to our hearts what winds are to the
sea. They grow into tempests, true; they are
sometimes even the cause of shipwrecks.
But the winds render the sea navigable, their
constant agitation of its surface is the cause of its
preservation, and if they are often dangerous, it is
for the pilot to know how to navigate in safety.

Moderate, therefore, your imprudent vivacity;
manifest less passion and you will excite more
in her heart. We do not appreciate the worth of
a prize more than when we are on the point of
losing it. Some regulation in matters of love are
indispensable for the happiness of both parties.

Ninon de l'Enclos

The human heart is an insolvable enigma. It is a whimsical combination of all the known contrarieties. We think we know its workings; we see their effects; we ignore the cause.

The words you burned to hear have been pronounced. More, she has allowed to escape her a thousand involuntary proofs of the passion you have inspired. Far from diminishing your love, the certainty that you are beloved in return has increased it; in a word, you are the happiest of men.

Gotthold Ephraim Lessing

Equality is the firmest bond of love.

Henry Wadsworth Longfellow

Like Dian's kiss, unasked, unsought,
Love gives itself, but is not bought;
    Nor voice, nor sound betrays
    Its deep, impassioned gaze.

That was the first sound in the song of love!
Scarce more than silence is, and yet a sound.
Hands of invisible spirits touch the strings
Of that mysterious instrument, the soul,
And play the prelude of our fate. We hear
The voice prophetic, and are not alone.

Richard Lovelace

If I have freedom in my love,
And in my soul am free,
Angels alone that soar above,
Enjoy such liberty.

Let others Glory follow,
In their false riches wallow,
And with their grief be merry;
Leave me but Love and Sherry.

Lucasta frown and let me die,
    But smile and see I live;
The sad indifference of your Eye
    Both kills, and doth reprieve.

Richard Lovelace

> Vain dreams of love, that only so much bliss
> Allow us as to know our wretchedness;
> And deal a larger measure in our pain
> By showing joy, then hiding it again.

Amy Lowell

> I would choose
> To lead him in a maze along the patterned paths,
> A bright and laughing maze for my heavy-booted
>   lover.
> Till he caught me in the shade,
> And the buttons of his waistcoat bruised my
> body as he clasped me,
> Aching, melting, unafraid.
>
> . . . Love weaves odd fancies in a lonely place.

Amy Lowell

> She did not want the locket, yet she did.
> To have him love her she found very sweet,
> But it is hard to keep love always hid.

Christopher Marlowe

> Come, live with me and be my love,
> And we will all the pleasures prove.
> That hills and valleys, dales and fields,
> Woods or steepy mountain yields.

Andrew Marvell

So we alone the happy, rest,
　　Whilst all the world is poor,
And have within ourselves possessed
　　All Love's and Nature's store.

Therefore the love which us doth bind,
But Fate so enviously debars,
Is the conjunction of the mind,
And opposition of the stars.

Think'st thou that this love can stand,
　　Whilst thou still dost say me nay?
Love unpaid does soon disband:
　　Love binds love, as hay binds hay.

Claude McKay

And we will build a lonely nest
Beside an open glade,
And there forever will we rest,
O love—O nut-brown maid!

But you have torn a nerve out of my frame,
A gut that no physician can replace,
And reft my life of happiness and aim.
Oh what new purpose shall I now embrace?
What substance hold, what lovely form pursue,
When my thought burns through everything to
   you?

Your voice is the color of a robin's breast,
And there's a sweet sob in it like rain—still rain in
   the night.

George Meredith

I speak of love, not the mask, and not of the flutings upon the theme of love, but of the passion; a flame, having, like our mortality, death in it as well as life, that may or may not be lasting.

There is no direr disaster in love than the death of imagination.

Edna St. Vincent Millay

After all, my erstwhile dear,
   My no longer cherished,
Need we say it was not love,
   Now that love is perished?

Life is a quest and love a quarrel—

My heart is what it was before,
   A house where people come and go
But it is winter with your love,
   The sashes are beset with snow.

John Milton

How can I live without thee, how forego
Thy sweet converse, and love so dearly join'd,
To live again in these wild woods forlorn?

. . . thus these two,
Imparadis'd in one another's arms,
The happier Eden, shall enjoy their fill
Of bliss on bliss . . .

Lady Mary Wortley Montagu

Be plain in dress, and sober in your diet;
In short, my deary, kiss me, and be quiet.

Michel de Montaigne

Love founds itself wholly upon pleasure, and
indeed has it more full, lively, and stinging; a
pleasure inflamed by difficulty; there must be in
it sting and ardour; 'tis no more love, if without
darts and fire.

Thomas Moore

A boat at midnight sent alone
To drift upon the moonless sea,
A lute, whose leading chord is gone,
A wounded bird, that hath but one
Imperfect wing to soar upon,
    Are like what I am without thee!

If I speak to thee in Friendship's name,
    Thou think'st I speak too coldly;
If I mention Love's devoted flame,
    Thou say'st I speak too boldly.
Between these two unequal fires,
    Why doom me thus to hover?
I'm a friend, if such thy heart requires,
    If more thou seek'st, a lover.

Alfred Noyes

I'll come to thee by moonlight, though
hell should bar the way.

Ovid

Every lover is a soldier, and Cupid has a camp of his own.

Jupiter, from on high, smiles at the perjuries of lovers, and commands the Aeolian south winds to sweep them away as worthless. Jupiter was accustomed to swear falsely to Juno by the Styx; now is he himself indulgent to his own precedent.

Take care that no one loves you in security, without a rival; love is not very lasting if you remove all rivalry.

Blaise Pascal

In love, silence is of more avail than speech. It is good to be abashed; there is an eloquence in silence that penetrates more deeply than language can. How well a lover persuades his mistress when he is abashed before her, who elsewhere has so much presence of mind!

Blaise Pascal

Let us not therefore exclude reason from love, since they are inseparable. The poets were not right in painting Love blind; we must take off his bandage and restore to him henceforth the enjoyment of his eyes.

Respect and love should be so well proportioned as to sustain each other without love being stifled by respect.

We are born with a disposition to love in our hearts, which is developed in proportion as the mind is perfected, and impels us to love what appears to us beautiful without ever having been told what this is. Who can doubt after this whether we are in the world for anything else than to love? In fact, we conceal in vain, we always love.

Blaise Pascal

Whatever compass of mind one may have, he is capable of only one great passion; hence, when love and ambition are found together, they are only half as great as they would be if only one of them existed.

William Penn

Between a man and his wife nothing ought to rule but love.

Never marry but for love; but see that thou lovest what is lovely. If love be not thy chiefest motive, thou wilt soon grow weary of a married state, and stray from thy promise, to search out thy pleasures in forbidden places.

James Robinson Planché

'Tis said that marriages are made above,
And so perhaps a few may be by love;
But from this smell of brimstone I should say
They must be making matches here all day!

Li Po

He is out on the South Lake,
Gathering white lilies.
The lotus flowers seem to whisper love,
And fill the boatman's heart with sadness.

In the tiger-striped gold case he left for her
    keeping
There remains a pair of white-feathered arrows
Amid the cobwebs and dust gathered of long
    years—
Oh, empty tokens of love, too sad to look upon!
She takes them out and burns them to ashes.

Li Po

Swallows, two by two,—always two by two.
A pair of swallows are an envy for man.

Edgar Allan Poe

We loved with a love that was more than
   love—
     I and my Annabel Lee;
With a love that the winged seraphs of
   heaven
     Coveted her and me.

Being everything which now thou art,
   Be nothing which thou art not.
So with the world thy gentle ways,
   Thy grace, thy more than beauty,
Shall be an endless theme of praise,
   And love—a simple duty.

Maria Louise Pool

Rheumatism and love keep a man awake.

Alexander Pope

Ah! beauteous maid! let this example move
Your mind, averse from all the joys of love.
Deign to be lov'd, and every heart subdue!
What nymph could e'er attract such crowds as
    you?

How oft, when pressed to marriage, have I said,
Curse on all laws but those which love has made?
Love, free as air, at sight of human ties,
Spreads his light wings, and in a moment flies.

Alexander Pope

Ye gods! and is there no relief for love?
But soon the sun with milder rays descends
To the cool ocean, where his journey ends.
On me Love's fiercer flames for ever prey,
By night he scorches, as he burns by day.

Matthew Prior

Love is a jest, and vows are wind.

She soothes, but never can enthrall my mind:
Why may not peace and love for once be join'd?

Alexander Pushkin

O Love, O Love,
O hear my prayer:
Again send me
Those visions thine,
And on the morrow
Raptured anew
Let me die
Without awaking!

Walter Raleigh

If all the world and Love were young,
And truth in every shepherd's tongue,
Those pretty pleasures might me move
To live with thee, and be thy love.

Samuel Richardson

"Your observation, my dear, is just," replied
Mr. B., "and though I am confident the lady was
more in earnest than myself in the notion of
Platonic love, yet am I convinced, and always
was, that Platonic love is Platonic nonsense; 'tis
the fly buzzing about the blaze, till its wings are
scorched . . . "

Samuel Richardson

What snivelers, what dotards, when they suffer themselves to be run away with by it!—An unpermanent passion! Since, if (ashamed of its more proper name) we must call it love, love gratified is love satisfied—and love satisfied is indifference begun.

Yet the woman who resents not initiatory freedoms must be lost. For love is an encroacher. Love never goes backward. Love is always aspiring. Always must aspire. Nothing but the highest act of love can satisfy an indulged love. And what advantage has a lover who values not breaking the peace, over his mistress who is felicitous to keep it!

Christina Georgina Rossetti

My heart is like a singing bird
Whose nest is in a watered shoot:
My heart is like an apple-tree
Whose boughs are bent with thickset fruit . . .

Why strive for love when love is o'er—
Why bind a restive heart?

Edmond Rostand

Come, do not despond! Love is a lottery.

Trust to the blindness of love . . . and vanity!

Nicholas Rowe

Love is, or ought to be, our greatest bliss;
Since every other joy, how dear soever,
Gives way to that, and we leave all for Love.

Nicholas Rowe

O love! how are thy precious, sweetest minutes
Thus ever cross'd, thus vex'd with disappointments!
Now pride, now fickleness, fantastic quarrels,
And sullen coldness give us pains by turns . . .

Helen Rowland

Between lovers a little confession is a dangerous thing.

Love is like a good dinner; the only way to get any satisfaction out of it is to enjoy it while it lasts, have no regrets when it is over and pay the price with good grace.

Tobacco and love and olives are all acquired tastes; your first smoke makes you sick, your first olive tastes bitter, and your first love affair makes you unhappy.

Variety is the spice of love.

George Sand (Amandine Dupin, Baroness Dudevant)

But beneath my mask, I have preserved a free soul, and since I had the command of my reason, have resolved never to marry but where I love.

Happily, the prayers of a lover are more imperious than the menaces of the whole earth, and even than the terrors of conscience.

Carl Sandburg

Love goes far. Here love ends.
Have me in the blue and the sun.

Sappho

'Twas this deprived my soul of rest,
And raised such tumults in my breast;
For while I gazed, in transport tossed,
My breath was gone, my voice was lost.

Friedrich von Schiller

> Ah, to that far distant strand
>   Bridge there was not to convey,
> Not a bark was near at hand,
>   Yet true love soon found the way.
>
> Why teach that love is nought but trifling vain?
>   Why cavil at our youthful joyous play?
> Thou art benumbed in winter's icy chain,
>   And yet canst view with scorn the golden May!

Walter Scott

> Love rules the court, the camp, the grove,
> And man below, and saints above;
> For love is heaven, and heaven is love.

William Shakespeare

And, when Love speaks, the voice of all the gods,
Makes heaven drowsy with the harmony.

Ay, me! for aught that I ever could read,
Could ever hear by tale or history,
The course of true love never did run smooth.

But love is blind, and lovers cannot see
The pretty follies that themselves commit.

By heaven, I do love; and it hath taught me to
rhyme, and to be melancholy . . .

William Shakespeare

Haply I think on thee,—and then my state
(Like to the lark at break of day arising
From sullen earth) sings hymns at heaven's gate;
    For thy sweet love remember'd, such wealth
       brings,
    That I scorn to change my state with kings.

Love sought is good, but given unsought is
better.

My bounty is as boundless as the sea,
My love as deep: the more I give to thee,
The more I have, for both are infinite.

O, that I were a glove upon that hand,
That I might touch that cheek!

She is mine own,
And I as rich in having such a jewel
As twenty seas, if all their sand were pearl.

George Bernard Shaw

Believe me, love is an overrated passion; it would be irremediably discredited but that young people, and the romancers who live upon their follies, have a perpetual interest in rehabilitating it.

I am only an unromantic gentleman, hiding from a romantic lady who is in love with me.

I am trying to offend you in order to save myself from falling in love with you; and I have not the heart to let myself succeed. On your life, do not listen to me or believe me: I have no right to say these things to you. Some fiend enters into me when I am at your side.

The fickleness of women I love is only equaled by the infernal constancy of the women who love me.

George Bernard Shaw

> Well, for five weeks I have walked and talked and
> dallied with the loveliest woman in the world;
> and the upshot is that I am flying from her, and
> am for a hermit's cave until I die. Love cannot
> keep possession of me; all my strongest powers
> rise up against it and will not endure it.

Percy Bysshe Shelley

> . . . Love, from its awful throne of patient power
> In the wise heart, from the last giddy hour
>   Of dread and endurance, from the slippery,
>   steep,
> And narrow verge of crag-like agony, springs
> And folds over the world its healing wings.

Percy Bysshe Shelley

Love withers under constraint: its very essence is
liberty: it is compatible neither with obedience,
jealousy, nor fear: it is there most pure, perfect,
and unlimited, where its votaries live in
confidence, equality and unreserved.

Philip Sidney

My true love hath my heart, and I have his,
By just exchange, one for the other given:
I hold his dear, and mine he cannot miss,
There never was a better bargain driven.

Song of Solomon 8:6

Set me as a seal upon thine heart, as a seal upon
thine arm: for love is strong as death; jealousy is
cruel as the grave: the coals thereof are coals of
fire, which hath a most vehement flame.

Edmund Spenser

My verse your vertues rare shall eternize,
And in the hevens wryte your glorious name.
Where, when as death shall all the world
subdew,
Our love shall live, and later life renew.

Anne Louise Germaine de Staël (Madame de Staël)

Love is the emblem of eternity: it confounds all
notion of time: effaces all memory of a beginning,
all fear of an end: we fancy that we have always
possessed what we love, so difficult is it to imagine
how we could have lived without it.

Nothing in love can be premeditated; it is as a
power divine, that thinks and feels within us,
unswayed by our control.

Anne Louise Germaine de Staël (Madame de Staël)

Unhappy love freezes all our affections: our own
soul grows inexplicable to us. More than we
gained while we were happy, we lose by
the reverse.

Stendhal (Marie-Henri Beyle)

A generous woman would lay down her life a thousand times for her lover, yet would break with him for ever on a trivial point of pride as to whether the door should be left open or shut.

A whirling waltz in a drawing-room lit by a thousand candles will set young hearts afire, banish shyness, bring a new awareness of strength, and in the end give *the courage to love*.

Stendhal (Marie-Henri Beyle)

All unsuspectingly, a man who is really in love says the most delightful things, and speaks in a language unknown to him.

If you are perfectly natural there will be a complete fusion of the happiness of both of you. Because of fellow-feeling and various other laws which govern our natures, this is, quite simply, the greatest happiness that can exist.

In love, unlike most other passions, the recollection of what you have had and lost is always better than what you can hope for in the future.

Love is like a fever which comes and goes quite independently of the will.

The loves of two people in love with each other are seldom the same. Passionate love has its phases, when first one partner and then the other will be more in love.

Stendhal (Marie-Henri Beyle)

It has been borne upon me this evening that perfect music has the same effect on the heart as the presence of the beloved. It gives, in fact, apparently more intense pleasure than anything else on earth. If everyone reacted to music as I do, nothing would ever induce men to fall in love.

The sight of anything beautiful, in Nature or the arts, makes you think instantly of your beloved.

The whole art of loving seems to me, in a nutshell, to consist in saying precisely what the degree of intoxication requires at any given moment. In other words, you must listen to your heart. You must not think this is easy: if you are truly in love and your lover says things which make you happy, you will lose the power of speech.

Stendhal (Marie-Henri Beyle)

To love is to enjoy seeing, touching, and sensing with all the senses, as closely as possible, a lovable object which loves in return.

When heaven has endowed you with a soul made for love, not to love is to deprive yourself and others of great happiness. It is as if an orange-tree dared not flower for fear of committing a sin.

Laurence Sterne

. . . for Love an please your Honor, is exactly like war, in this; That a soldier, though he has escaped three weeks complete o' Saturday night,—may nevertheless be shot through his heart on Sunday morning.

John Suckling

The sea's my mind, which calm would be,
Were it from winds (my passions) free;
But out alas! no sea I find
Is troubled like a lover's mind.

Out upon it! I have lov'd
Three whole days together;
And am like to love three more,
If it prove fair weather.

Why so pale and wan, fond lover?
Prithee, why so pale?
Will, when looking well can't move her,
Looking ill prevail?

Jonathan Swift

In all I wish how happy should I be,
Thou grand Deluder, were it not for thee?
So weak thou art, that fools thy power
    despise;
And yet so strong, thou triumph'st o'er the
    wise.
Thy traps are laid with such peculiar art,
They catch the cautious; let the rash depart.

Love, why do we one passion call;
When 'tis a compound of them all;
Where hot and cold, where sharp and sweet,
In all their equipages meet:
Where pleasures mix'd with pains appear,
Sorrow with joy, and hope with fear . . .

Algernon Charles Swinburne

> And the best and the worst of this is
> That neither is most to blame,
> If you've forgotten my kisses,
> And I've forgotten your name.

Torquato Tasso

> Let us love, for the life of Man has no truce with years, and is still consuming; let us love, for the sun dies, and is born again; our short light sets from us, and sleep brings on eternal night.

> Perhaps, if you had tasted but once the thousandth part of the joys which an amorous heart feels in the return of mutual love, you would say, repenting with a sigh, Lost is all the time that is not spent in Love: Alas, my ill-spent youth!

Sara Teasdale

. . . Come, then, and let us walk
Since we have reached the park. It is our garden,
All black and blossomless this winter night,
But we bring April with us, you and I;
We set the whole world on the trail of spring.

The tree of my song stands bare
    Against the blue—
I gave my songs to the rest,
    Myself to you.

There is no magic any more,
    We meet as other people do,
You work no miracle for me
    Nor I for you.

The people on the street look up at us
All envious. We are a king and queen,
Our royal carriage is a motor bus,
We watch our subjects with a haughty joy . . .

Alfred, Lord Tennyson

Let love be free; free love is for the best:
And, after heaven, on our dull side of death,
What should be best, if not so pure a love
Clothed in so pure a loveliness?

And he that shuts out Love, in turn shall be
Shut out from Love, and on her threshold lie,
Howling in outer darkness.

Terence

Good gods! What sort of disease is this? Is it
possible a man should be so perfectly changed by
love that you cannot know him to be the same?
No one was less guilty of folly than this master of
mine, nor was any one more discreet, or more a
master of his passions.

So as I tell you: the falling out of lovers is the
renewal of love.

William Makepeace Thackeray

Almost all women will give a sympathizing hearing to men who are in love. Be they ever so old, they grow young again in conversation, and renew their own early time.

Theocritus

For oft the foul, good Polypheme, is fair in the eyes of love.

Henry David Thoreau

Love is the wind, the tide, the waves, the sunshine. Its power is incalculable; it is many horse-power. It never ceases, it never slacks; it can move the globe without a resting-place; it can warm without fire; it can feed without meat; it can clothe without garments; it can shelter without roof; it can make a paradise within which will dispense with a paradise without.

Henry David Thoreau

In love and friendship the imagination is as much exercised as the heart; and if either is outraged the other will be estranged. It is commonly the imagination which is wounded first, rather than the heart,—it is so much more sensitive.

Love is a severe critic. Hate can pardon more than love. They who aspire to love worthily subject themselves to an ordeal more rigid than any other.

Leo Tolstoy

Do I regret what I have done? No, no, no! If it were all to do again from the beginning, it would be the same. For us, for you and for me, there is only one thing that matters, whether we love each other. Other people need not consider. Why are we living here apart and not seeing each other? Why can't I go? I love you, and I don't care for anything . . .

He knew she was there by the rapture and the terror that seized on his heart. She was standing talking to a lady at the opposite end of the ground. There was apparently nothing striking either in her dress or her attitude. But for Levin she was as easy to find in that crowd, as a rose among nettles. Everything was made bright by her.

Leo Tolstoy

She waited for a long while without moving, and had forgotten about him. She thought of that other; she pictured him, and felt how her heart was flooded with emotion and guilty delight at the thought of him.

Anthony Trollope

A man in love seldom loves less because his love becomes difficult.

A man's love, till it has been chastened and fastened by the feeling of duty which marriage brings with it, is instigated mainly by the difficulty of pursuit.

Come, come, Mr. Arabin, don't let love interfere with your appetite. It never does with mine.

Anthony Trollope

Her love to her was the same as her religion. When it was once acknowledged by her to be a thing good and trustworthy, all the world might know it. Was it not a glory to her that he had chosen her, and why should she conceal her glory?

It is seldom that a young man may die from a broken heart; but if an old man have a heart still left to him, it is more fragile.

Men will love to the last, but they love what is fresh and new. A woman's love can live on the recollection of the past, and cling to what is old and ugly.

There is no happiness in love, except at the end of an English novel.

To be alone with the girl to whom he is not engaged is a man's delight; to be alone with the man to whom she is engaged is the woman's.

Virgil

In Hell, and Earth, and Seas, and Heav'n above,
Love conquers all; and we must yield to Love.

Hugh Walpole

It is a platitude, of course, to say that there is
probably no one alive who does not remember
some occasion of a sudden communion with
another human being that was so beautiful, so
touching, so transcendentally above human
affairs that a revelation was the only definition
for it. Afterwards, when analysis plays its part,
one may talk about physical attractions, about
common intellectual interests, about spiritual
bonds, about what you please, but one knows
that the essence of that meeting is undefined.

John Hall Wheelock

> What of good and evil,
> Hell, and Heaven above—
> Trample them with love!
> Ride over them with love!

Walt Whitman

I give you my love, more precious than
  money,
I give you myself before preaching or law:
Will you give me yourself? will you come
  travel with me?
Shall we stick by each other as long as we
  live?

Walt Whitman

I see the vast alembic ever working—I see and
    know the flames that heat the world;
The glow, the blush, the beating hearts of lovers,
So blissful happy some—and some so silent,
    dark, and nigh to death:
Love, that is all the earth to lovers—Love, that
    mocks time and space,
Love, that is day and night—Love, that is sun
    and moon and stars,
Love, that is crimson, sumptuous, sick with
    perfume:
No other words but words of love—no other
    thought but Love.

Ella Wheeler Wilcox

Let the love-word sound in the listening ear,
Nor wait to speak it above a bier.
Oh, the time for telling your love is brief,
But long, long, long is the time for grief . . .
Are you loving enough?

Oscar Wilde

Hearts live by being wounded. Pleasure may turn a heart to stone, riches may make it callous, but sorrow—oh, sorrow cannot break it.

Men always want to be a woman's first love. That is their clumsy vanity. We women have a more subtle instinct about things. What we like is to be a man's last romance.

The London season is entirely matrimonial; people are either hunting for husbands or hiding from them.

Oscar Wilde

. . . the people who love only once in their lives
are the really shallow people. What they call
their loyalty, and their fidelity, I call either the
lethargy of custom or their lack of imagination.

The proper basis for marriage is a mutual
misunderstanding.

The very essence of romance is uncertainty.

There is always something ridiculous about the
emotions of people whom one has ceased to love.

Those who are faithful know only the trivial
side of love: it is the faithless who know love's
tragedies.

You want a new excitement, Prince. Let me see—
you have been married twice already; suppose
you try—falling in love for once.

Oscar Wilde

What a silly thing love is! It is not half as useful as logic, for it does not prove anything and it is always telling one things that are not going to happen, and making one believe things that are not true.

When one is in love one begins by deceiving oneself. And one ends by deceiving others. That's what the world calls a romance. But a really *grande passion* is comparatively rare now-a-days. It is the privilege of people who have nothing to do.

Who on earth writes to him on pink paper? It looks like the beginning of a middle-class romance. Romance should never begin with sentiment. It should begin with science and end with a settlement.

William Carlos Williams

I have never or seldom said, my dear I love you,
when I would rather say: My dear, I wish you
were in Tierra del Fuego.
Love is so precious

my townspeople
that if I were you I would
have it under lock and key—
like the air or the Atlantic or
like poetry!

Nathaniel Parker Willis

True love is at home on a carpet,
And mightily likes his ease—
And true love has an eye for a dinner,
And starves beneath shady trees.
His wing is the fan of a lady,
His foot's an invisible thing,
And his arrow is tipp'd with a jewel
And shot from a silver string.

Mary Wollstonecraft

I must love and admire with warmth, or I sink into sadness.

It is far better to be often deceived than never to trust; to be disappointed in love than never to love; to love a husband's fondness than forfeit his esteem.

William Wordsworth

True beauty dwells in deep retreats,
    Whose veil is unremoved
'Till heart with heart in concord beats,
    And the lover is beloved.

What fond and wayward thoughts will slide
Into a lover's head!

Mary Wroth

Love, a child, is ever crying;
Please him, and he straight is flying;
Give him, he the more is craving,
Never satisfied with having.

Ann Yearsley

> Then, whilst thy eager charming eyes
> Run o'er these lines, may love arise
> Within thy breast to equal mine,
> Nor read in vain my Valentine.

William Butler Yeats

Down by the salley gardens my love and I
  did meet;
She passed the salley gardens with little
  snow-white feet.
She bid me take love easy, as the leaves
  grown on the tree;
But I, being young and foolish, with her
  would not agree.

William Butler Yeats

How many loved your moments of glad grace,
And loved your beauty with love false or true;
But one man loved the pilgrim soul in you,
And loved the sorrows of your changing face.

Oh, love is the crooked thing,
There is nobody wise enough
To find out all that is in it,
For he would be thinking of love
Till the stars had run away,
And the shadows eaten the moon.

List of Works

Page 48. John Singer Sargent (1856–1925). *A Morning Walk*, 1888.

Page 54. Benjamin West (1738–1820). *Cupid and Psyche*, 1808.

Page 58. Gustav Klimt (1862–1918). *The Kiss*, 1907–08.

Page 70. François Boucher (1703–1770). *A Pastoral Landscape with a Shepherd and Shepherdess Seated by Ruins*, c. 1730.

Page 78. John William Waterhouse (1849–1917). *Tristram and Isolde*, 1916.

Page 84. Anonymous. *A Bridal Pair*, c. 1470.

Page 88. Lucas Cranach the Elder (1472–1553). *Samson and Delilah*, c. 1529.

Page 94. Paris Bordon (1500–1571). *Venus, Mars, and Cupid Crowned by Victory*, c. 1550.

Page 98. Pierre-August Cot (1837–1883). *The Storm*, 1880.

Page 102. William Chadwick (1879–1962). *On the Porch*, c. 1908.

Page 106. Eva Gonzales (1849–1883). *Morning Awakening*, 1877–78.

Page 110. Jan van Eyck (c. 1395–1441). *Portrait of Giovanni Arnolfini and His Wife*, 1434.